9.95

GW00455301

Published 2005
© International Music Publications Ltd
Griffin House 161 Hammersmith Road
London W6 8BS England

Music arranged and engraved by Artemis Music Ltd
(www.artemismusic.com)

Reproducing this music in any form is illegal and forbidden
by the Copyright, Designs and Patents Act, 1988

Against All Odds (Take A Look At Me Now)

Words and Music by Phil Collins

© 1984 EMI Golden Torch Music Corp, EMI United Partnership Ltd, USA and Hit And Run Music (Publishing) Ltd
Worldwide print rights controlled by Warner Bros. Publications Inc/IMP Ltd and Hit & Run Music (Publishing) Ltd, London WC2H 0QY

The Blower's Daughter

Words and Music by Damien Rice

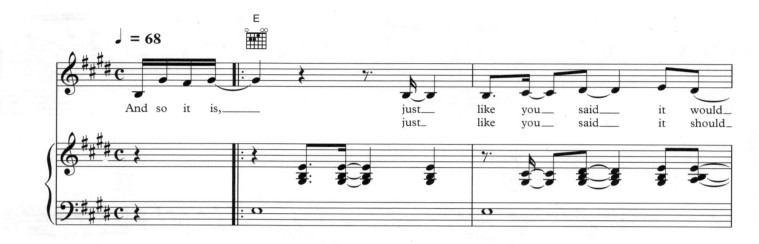

And so it is,_____ just__ like you__ said__ it would__
just__ like you__ said__ it should__

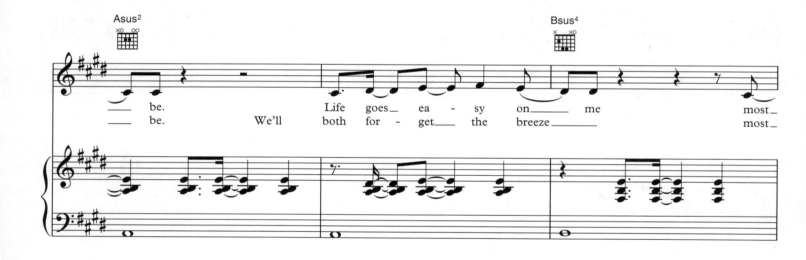

___ be. Life goes__ ea - sy on_____ me most__
___ be. We'll both for - get__ the breeze_____ most_

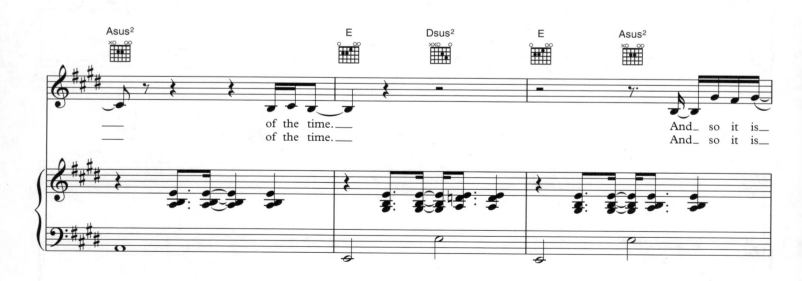

___ of the time.__ And_ so it is__
___ of the time.__ And_ so it is

© 2003 Warner/Chappell Music Publishing Ltd, London W6 8BS

Boulevard Of Broken Dreams

Words and Music by Billy Joe Armstrong, Michael Pritchard and Frank Wright

© 2004 Green Daze Music, USA
Warner/Chappell North America Ltd, London W6 8BS

CODA

walk a - lone.__

Club Foot

Words and Music by Sergio Pizzorno and Christopher Karloff

C'mon take con-trol___ of me, you're mess-ing with the en-e-my. Said it's
Friends take con-trol___ of me, stalk-ing 'cross the gal-le-ry. All these

© 2004 EMI Music Publishing Ltd, London WC2H 0QY

Do Something

Words and Music by Angela Hunte, Christian Karlsson and Pontus Winnberg

© 2002 Masani El Shabazz, Foray Music and Murlyn Songs AB, Sweden
EMI Music Publishing Ltd, London WC2H 0QY and Universal Music Publishing Ltd, London SW6 4LZ

like... Some-bod - y pass my gui - tar_____ so I can look like a star_

Pre-chorus:

____ _and spend this cash_ _like..._

What - cha gon - na do when the crowd goes, "Ay oh"?_____

Why y'all stand - ing on the wall? Mu - sic's fall - in' ev - 'ry - where,_

Verse 2:
Now, you're all in my grill
'Cause I say what I feel,
Only rock to what's real.
Never with a bum, bum.
But I can't do that with you.
Already here with my crew.
You can roll if you can,
Don't be a punk, punk.
(To Pre-chorus:)

Everlasting Love

Words and Music by Buzz Cason and Mac Gayden

Heart's gone a-stray___ deep_ in hurt_____ when they_ go.___

___ I went a-way,___ just___ when you

© 1967 Rising Sons Music Inc, USA
Peter Maurice Music Co Ltd, London WC2H 0QY

Get Right

Words and Music by James Brown, Rich Harrison and Usher Raymond

© 2005 Dynatone Publishing Co, EMI Blackwood Music Inc, Dam Rich Music, EMI April Music Inc and Ur-IV, USA
Intersong Music Ltd, London W6 8BS and EMI Music Publishing Ltd, London WC2H 0QY
[This song contains a sample from "Soul Power 74" by Brown © Dynatone Publishing Co]

I Got You Babe

Words and Music by Sonny Bono

"Hey Patsy, you ready?" "I'm ready Avid" "Davina?" "I'm ready" "Ok my babies, shut up and sing" They

— say we're young and we don't know,— we won't find out un-til—— we—
They say our love won't pay the rent,— be-fore it's earned our mon-ey's all been

— grow.
spent.

Well I don't know— if all that's true, 'cause
I guess that's so, we don't have a pot, but at

© 1965 (renewed) Cotillion Music Inc and Chris Marc Music, USA
Warner/Chappell Music Ltd, London W6 8BS

44

Is The Way To Amarillo

Words and Music by Neil Sedaka and Howard Greenfield

© 1971 Kirshner Songs Inc, USA
Kirshner-Warner Bros. Music Ltd, London W6 8BS

If There's Any Justice

Words and Music by Mick Leeson and Peter Vale

© 1999 EMI Virgin Music Ltd, London WC2H 0QY and Notting Hill Music (UK) Ltd, London W8 4AP

Karma

Words and Music by Alicia Augello-Cook, Kerry Brothers and Taneisha Smith

Moderately slow

Weren't you ___ the one ___ that said ___ that you ___ don't want ___ me an - y - more, ___
And when ___ you came ___ home you'd ___ al - ways ___ have some ___ sor - ry ___ ex - cuse, ___

© 2003 Lellow Productions Inc, Book Of Daniel Music, Krucialkeys2life Music, Taneisha Smith Music and EMI April Music Inc, USA
EMI Music Publishing Ltd, London WC2H 0QY

down.) Now ___ who's cry - in,' ___ de - sir - in' ___ to come back ___ to me? ___

Lose My Breath

Words and Music by Garrett Hamler, Rodney Jerkins, Lashawn Daniels,
Carter, Beyonce Knowles, Fred Jerkins III, Kelendria Rowland and Michelle Williams

Can you keep up ba - by boy?__ (Make me lose my breath). Bring the noise.__

__ (Make me lose my breath). Hit me hard.__ (Make me lose my huh huh huh huh).

Can you keep up ba - by boy?__ (Make me lose my breath). Bring the noise.__

© 2004 Christopher Garrett's, Hitco South, Rodney Jerkins Productions Inc, Lashawn Daniels Productions Inc, Carter Boys Publishing, EMI
Blackwood Music Inc, EMI April Music Inc, Fred Jerkins Publishing, USA and Copyright Control
EMI Music Publishing Ltd, London WC2H 0QY, Windswept Music (London) Ltd, London W6 9BD, Famous Music Publishing Ltd, London SW6 3JW
and Copyright Control

66

68

You don't have no bus-'ness in this, here's your pap-ers ba-by you are dis-missed.

Mary

Words and Music by Scott Hoffman and Jason Sellards

1. I love the tone that's in your laugh, gasp-ing for an ex-
2. I've had it ea - sy now, you see. When I'm down you're al-

- tra breath, wait-ing for the time to pass.
- ways there, stand-ing by to com - fort me.

© 2004 EMI Music Publishing Ltd, London WC2H 0QY

My Prerogative

Words and Music by Gene Griffin, Teddy Riley and Bobby Brown

Moderately ♩ = 100

People can take everything away from you,
But they can never take away your truth.
But the question is...
Can you handle mine?

Verse 1:
1. They say I'm craz - y. I real - ly don't care.

That's my pre - rog - a - tive.___ They say I'm nas - ty, but___ I

don't give a damn. Get - tin' boys is how I___ live.___ 2. Some ask me ques-

© 1988 EMI Virgin Songs Inc, Cal-Gene Music Inc, MCA-Unicity Music and Zomba Enterprises Inc, USA
EMI Music Publishing Ltd, London WC2H 0QY, Universal/MCA Music Ltd, London SW6 4LZ and Zomba Music Publishers, London SW6 3JW

Verses 2 & 3:

3. See additional lyrics

Verse 3:
Don't get me wrong,
I'm really not zooped.
Ego trips is not my thing.
All these strange relationships, really gets me down.
I see nothing wrong spreading myself around.
(To Chorus:)

Nothing Hurts Like Love

Words and Music by Diane Warren

1. Bro - ken hearts, bro - ken dreams. There's just some things that love brings. When you
2. So you gave all you had. How the sto - ry turned so sad. No - thing

learn that it's all been a lie, you cry. You find that
left but the tears in your eyes. You die in - side 'cause

© 2004 Realsongs, USA
EMI Music Publishing Ltd, London WC2H 0QY

82

The Reason

Words and Music by Douglas Robb, Daniel Estrin, Chris Hesse and Markku Lappalainen

I'm

not a   per - fect   per - son,_____   there's

sor - ry   that___ I   hurt___ you,_____   it's

© 2003 WB Music Corp and Spread Your Cheeks And Push Out The Music, USA
Warner/Chappell North America Ltd, London W6 8BS

ma - ny things I wish I did-n't do.
some-thing I must live with ev -'ry - day.

But
And

I con - ti - nue learn - ing
all the pain I put you through,

I
I

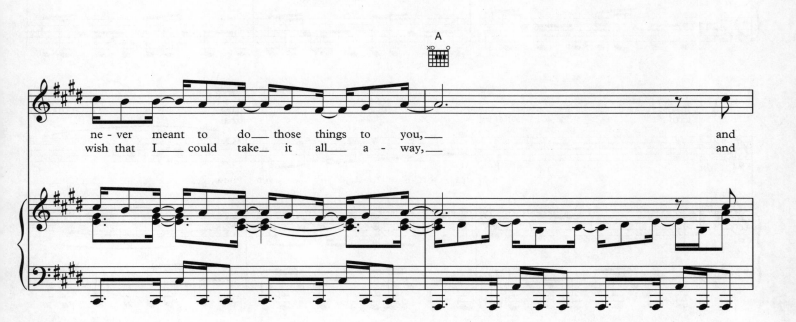

ne - ver meant to do those things to you,
wish that I could take it all a - way,

and
and

Room On The 3rd Floor

Words and Music by Thomas Fletcher and Daniel Jones

© 2004 Rashman Corp
Universal Music Publishing Ltd, London SW6 4LZ

Unwritten

Words and Music by Danielle Brisebois, Wayne Rodriques and Natasha Bedingfield

I am un - writ - ten, can't read my mind,___ I'm un - de - fined..
I break tra - di - tion, some-times my tries___ are out - side the line.__

I'm just___ be - gin - ning, the pen's in my hand,___
We've been___ con - di - tioned to not make mis - takes,__

© 2003 Gator Baby Music, EMI Blackwood Music Inc, EMI Music Publishing Ltd and Copyright Control
EMI Music Publishing Ltd, London WC2H 0QY and Copyright Control

You've Got A Friend

Words and Music by Carole King

© 1971 Screen Gems-EMI Music Inc, USA
Screen Gems-EMI Music Ltd, London WC2H 0QY

Walkie Talkie Man

Words and Music by Brad Carter, Tyson Kennedy, Jared Wrennall, Jacob Adams and Tim Youngson

© 2004 Thirtysixninetynine LLC, USA
EMI Music Publishing Ltd, London WC2H 0QY

100 YEARS OF POPULAR MUSIC

IMP

International
MUSIC
Publications

IMP's Exciting New Series!

100 YEARS OF POPULAR MUSIC

Vol. 1 - 9817A

Vol. 1 - 9819A

9816A

Vol. 1 - 9821A

Vol. 1 - 9823A

Vol. 2 - 9818A

Vol. 2 - 9820A

Vol. 2 - 9822A

Vol. 2 - 9824A

IMP
International MUSIC Publications

IMP's Exciting New Series!